DISCOVER
AMERICA

MARYLAND

Rennay Craats

AV² provides enriched content that supplements and complements this book. Weigl's AV² books strive to create inspired learning and engage young minds in a total learning experience.

Your AV² Media Enhanced books come alive with...

Audio
Listen to sections of the book read aloud.

Key Words
Study vocabulary, and complete a matching word activity.

Video
Watch informative video clips.

Quizzes
Test your knowledge.

Embedded Weblinks
Gain additional information for research.

Slide Show
View images and captions, and prepare a presentation.

Try This!
Complete activities and hands-on experiments.

... and much, much more!

Go to www.av2books.com, and enter this book's unique code.

BOOK CODE

K 3 3 6 8 7 8

AV² by Weigl brings you media enhanced books that support active learning.

Published by AV² by Weigl
350 5th Avenue, 59th Floor
New York, NY 10118
Website: www.av2books.com

Library of Congress Cataloging-in-Publication Data
Names: Craats, Rennay., author.
Title: Maryland : the Old Line State / Rennay Craats.
Description: New York, NY : AV2 by Weigl, [2016] | Series: Discover America |
  Includes index.
Identifiers: LCCN 2015048006 (print) | LCCN 2015048322 (ebook) | ISBN
  9781489648754 (hard cover : alk. paper) | ISBN 9781489648761 (soft cover :
  alk. paper) | ISBN 9781489648778 (Multi-User eBook)
Subjects: LCSH: Maryland--Juvenile literature.
Classification: LCC F181.3 .C735 2016 (print) | LCC F181.3 (ebook) | DDC 975.2--dc23
LC record available at http://lccn.loc.gov/2015048006

Printed in the United States of America, in Brainerd, Minnesota
1 2 3 4 5 6 7 8 9 20 19 18 17 16

042016
040816

Project Coordinator Heather Kissock
Art Director Terry Paulhus

Photo Credits
Every reasonable effort has been made to trace ownership and to obtain permission to reprint copyright material. The publisher would be pleased to have any errors or omissions brought to their attention so that they may be corrected in subsequent printings. The publisher acknowledges Getty Images, Corbis Images, iStock, and Alamy as its primary image suppliers for this title.

DISCOVER AMERICA

MARYLAND

Contents

STATE TREE
White Oak

STATE BIRD
Baltimore Oriole

STATE DOG
Chesapeake Bay Retriever

STATE FLAG
Maryland

STATE FLOWER
Black-eyed Susan

STATE SEAL
Maryland

Nickname
The Old Line State

Motto
Fatti Machii Parole Femine
(Strong Deeds, Gentle Words)

Song
"Maryland, My Maryland,"
words by James Ryder Randall
and sung to the tune of
"O, Tannenbaum"

Population
(2010 Census) 5,773,552
Ranked 19th state

Entered the Union
April 28, 1788, as the 7th state

Capital
Annapolis

Discover Maryland

Maryland is sometimes called "America in Miniature," a nickname reflecting both its small size and its great **diversity**. Although it covers a land area of only 9,774 square miles and is the ninth-smallest state in the United States, Maryland contains a great variety of landscapes and lifestyles.

From mountains to beaches, outdoor recreation opportunity is abundant in Maryland. Rocks State Park features Kilgore Falls set in 855 acres of dense forest. Baltimore Harbor and National Harbor are centers of culture and family fun. There are also 2,500 scenic byways throughout Maryland, offering a unique way to see the state.

Maryland is known for its crab. The Maryland blue crab's scientific name, *Callinectes sapidus Rathbun*, translates to "beautiful swimmer that is savory." The blue crab is a major part of Maryland's tourism industry. Crabbing in the Chesapeake Bay also generates money for the state.

Baltimore is Maryland's largest city and has one of the busiest ports in the country. This leading industrial center lies at the head of the Patapsco River **estuary**, 15 miles north of Chesapeake Bay. Baltimore is a popular tourist destination and contains many historic sites.

A big part of Maryland's work force and economy is connected to the federal government. Many people who live in Bethesda, Fredrick, and Gaithersberg consider themselves to be living in a suburb of Washington, D.C. So many people commute from Maryland to Washington, D.C., that the nation's capital has 2.5 times more people during working hours in the city than it has at night.

The Land

The Potomac River spans four states, including Maryland, and drains into the Chesapeake Bay.

Maryland measures about **250 miles** from east to west, but at its narrowest point from north to south is less than **2 miles wide.**

The country's **first federal highway** was finished in 1837, and ran from **Cumberland, Maryland,** to **Vandalia, Illinois.**

Beginnings

In 1632, King Charles I of England gave the land that would become Maryland to Lord Baltimore. Lord Baltimore was a nobleman from Great Britain who used the land to establish a colony for Roman Catholics seeking religious freedom from the Church of England. Settlers arrived in 1634, and quickly established positive relationships with the Native Americans in the area.

The Treaty of Paris ended the American Revolutionary War on April 15, 1783.

Marylanders fought hard in the American Revolutionary War for United States Independence. Washington called the Maryland troops "The Maryland Line" for their reliability, and often gave them difficult tasks. The Treaty of Paris, which acknowledged the independence of the colonies, was signed in Annapolis, Maryland, in 1783.

On April 28, 1788, Maryland achieved statehood, becoming the seventh of the original thirteen colonies to join the Union. Its citizens welcomed this new freedom and the new government. In 1790, George Washington, as the first U.S. president, chose the District of Columbia to be built on land donated by Maryland and neighboring Virginia, as the new capital of the United States.

Where is
MARYLAND?

WEST VIRGINIA

Maryland covers a total area of 12,407 square miles, including 9,774 square miles of land and 2,633 square miles of water. About 70 percent of Maryland's water area lies along the coast, while the remainder is inland. Despite its small size, the state has nearly 3,200 miles of shoreline.

United States Map

Maryland

Alaska Hawai'i

VIRGINIA

MAP LEGEND
- ▢ Maryland
- ☆ Capital City
- ● Major City
- ⬛ Atlantic Coastal Plain
- 🌲 Cedarville State Forest
- ▢ Bordering States
- ▢ Water

N

SCALE   0 |————————————| 25 miles

1 Annapolis

Annapolis, the state capital, is not only the center of state government but also the home of the U.S. Naval Academy. Located about 25 miles south of Baltimore, Annapolis was named in honor of Princess Anne, who ruled Great Britain as Queen Anne in the early 1700s.

2 Frederick

Frederick was founded in 1745 along a tributary to the Monocacy River. With more than 65,000 residents, Frederick is one of Maryland's largest cities, second only to Baltimore. South of Frederick is the Monocacy National Battlefield. This National Park site commemorates a Civil War battle that stopped the South from capturing Washington, D.C.

PENNSYLVANIA

MARYLAND

2 → ● **Frederick**

DISTRICT
OF COLUMBIA

Annapolis ☆ ← **1**

DELAWARE

4

3

---

3 **Atlantic Coastal Plain**

Millions of years ago, large glaciers carved the land into beaches and mountains, and formed the Atlantic Coastal Plain. It runs from Florida all the way to New York, cutting straight through Maryland. The swampy land and rich soil make it a perfect preservation site for fossils.

4 **Cedarville State Forest**

Once the winter camping ground of the Piscataway Indians, today Cedarville State Forest is a protected national park. It has more than 19.5 miles of marked trails. Visitors can bike, hike, or ride horses along the scenic routes, and camp out among the trees.

Land Features

From east to west, Maryland has several different landscapes. A coastal plain merges into the rolling Piedmont Plateau. To the west of the plateau is a section of the Blue Ridge Mountains. Between those mountains and the Appalachian Mountains, in the far west of the state, lies the Cumberland Valley. The highest point in the state, at 3,360 feet, is Hoye Crest on Backbone Mountain, which is part of the Appalachian chain.

Chesapeake Bay is one of the state's most notable features. This body of water juts into the state from the south, giving Maryland a long shoreline. About 2,700 different species of plants and animals live in and around the bay, including many fish and waterfowl.

Blue Ridge Mountains

The Blue Ridge Mountains slice through western Frederick County, in the northern part of the state.

Chesapeake Bay

More than one-third of the nation's annual blue-crab catch comes from Chesapeake Bay.

Assateague

Assateague National Wildlife Refuge supports a population of more than 300 wild horses.

Potomac River

The Potomac River defines the border between Maryland and Virginia and drains more than 3,800 square miles of Maryland territory.

Climate

Maryland is hot and humid in the summer, while winters are usually mild. Most precipitation falls as rain, but snow is common in winter. Sometimes wind from passing hurricanes reaches the eastern coast of Maryland.

Maryland's summer temperature averages 74° Fahrenheit, and 35°F in the winter. The highest temperature ever recorded was 109°F on several dates in different locations. The lowest temperature was –40°F, at Oakland, on January 13, 1912.

Average Annual Precipitation Across Maryland

Hagerstown usually gets less annual precipitation than most other places in Maryland. What factors might account for the difference?

LEGEND

Average Annual Precipitation (in inches) 1961–1990

200 – 100.1

100 – 25.1

25 – 5 and less

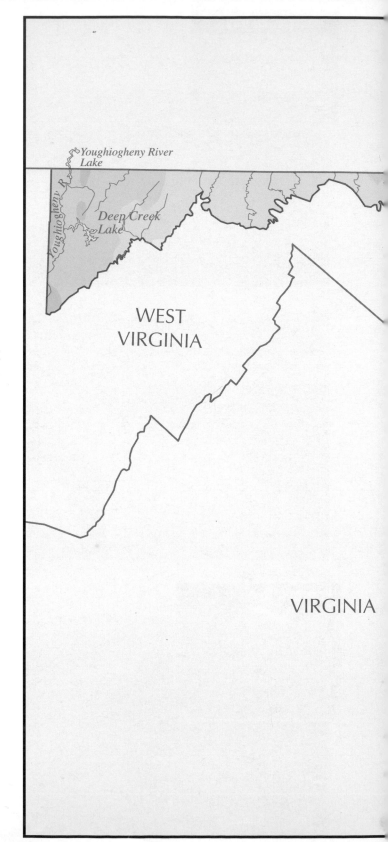

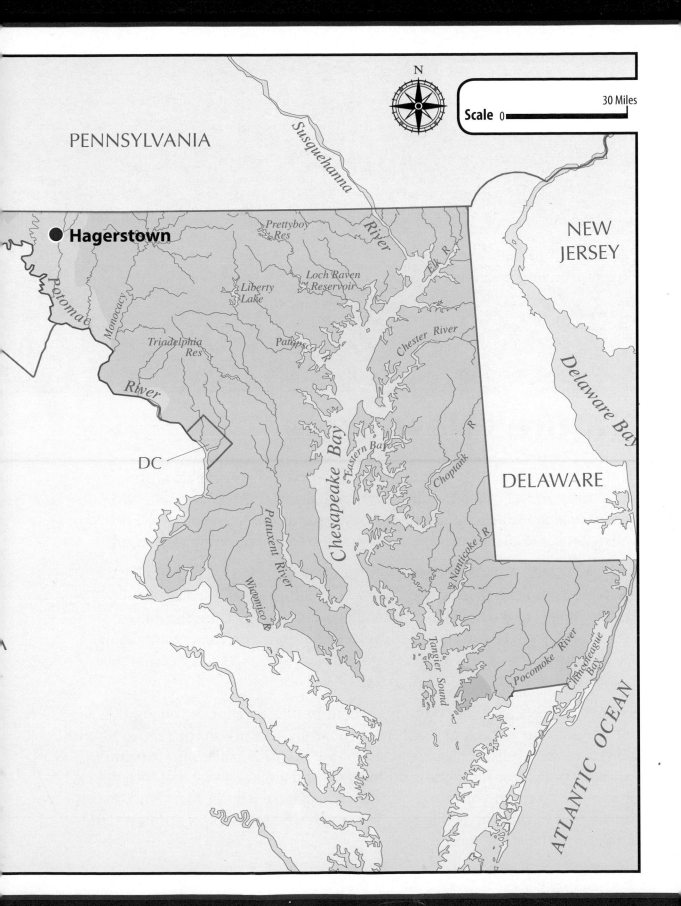

PENNSYLVANIA

Susquehanna River

Hagerstown

Potomac

NEW JERSEY

Prettyboy Res

Elk R

Monocacy

Loch Raven Reservoir

Liberty Lake

Chester River

Delaware Bay

Triadelphia Res

Patapsco R

River

DC

Chesapeake Bay

Eastern Bay

DELAWARE

Patuxent River

Choptank R

Wicomico R

Nanticoke R

Tangier Sound

Pocomoke River

Chincoteague Bay

ATLANTIC OCEAN

Maryland's timber provides the state with a $4-billion-a-year industry.

Nature's Resources

Important reserves of coal are found in Maryland's mountains. Miners dig most of the coal out of large pits called strip mines. The state also has limestone, sandstone, marble, granite, sand, and gravel mines. The construction industry uses these resources to make buildings and roads.

Water is another important natural resource in Maryland. The boundary between the upland plateau and the coastal plain is called the fall line. Where rivers cross the fall line, waterfalls occur. Energy from the falling water is harnessed to produce **hydroelectric** power. The Conowingo Dam serves both as a large hydroelectric power plant and as a bridge across the Susquehanna River.

Almost 40 percent of Maryland is covered in forests, which grow both hardwoods and softwoods. Each year, more than 2 million tons of wood are harvested, two-thirds of it hardwood. Some of this is made into furniture, cabinets, pallets, or lumber for buildings. Some of it is processed into paper, or shipped to paper plants out of state. The eastern part of Maryland does the most wood harvesting, while the majority of wood processing in Maryland happens in the west.

Maryland produces more than 2 million tons of coal each year.

Conowingo Dam is more than 4,000 feet long and 100 feet high. It was completed in 1928 and expanded in 1978.

Vegetation

Maryland has kept its beautiful forests largely intact. More than two-fifths of the state's land area is covered with forests, and more than half of the forested area has hardwood trees such as oaks and hickories. Black locust, black cherry, and ash trees are also common in the state. The dominant softwood tree is the loblolly pine.

Sweet gum and bald cypress trees flourish in the **wetlands** in the south. The wetlands, which cover about 600,000 acres, are home to thousands of other plants and animals. To the west, hemlock and white pine trees grow in the mountains.

Cypress Trees

Battle Creek Cypress Swamp is a 100-acre nature sanctuary in Calvert County.

White Oak

A mature white oak may produce up to 10,000 acorns annually.

Loblolly Pine

The loblolly pine typically stands between 90 and 110 feet tall but may reach heights of 150 feet or more.

Sweet Gum

The sweet gum tree produces "gumballs" which are more than an inch across, and turn from green to brown.

Wildlife

The forests are home to many different kinds of wildlife. Animals found in Maryland include white-tailed deer, black bears, wild turkeys, bald eagles, and orioles. The Delmarva fox squirrel, an **endangered species**, lives near Chesapeake Bay. Overdevelopment and competition for food have caused a decline in the number of these animals. They are found in wooded parts of Virginia and Maryland.

The Baltimore oriole, the official state bird, lives in Maryland's forests. The orange and black of the male's feathers are similar to the colors on the Calvert family crest. The bird takes its name from George Calvert, who was known as Lord Baltimore.

Maryland is home to some 27 species of snakes. Snakes found in the state include the green, corn, yellow rat, milk, king, and garter. Only two species are venomous, the northern copperhead and timber rattlesnake, which are both species of pit viper.

Bald Eagle

The Chesapeake Bay Environmental Center takes care of injured or orphaned bald eagles until they can released into nature.

Wild Turkeys

A recent survey counted about 5,000 wild turkeys in Maryland.

Northern Copperhead

Rarely more than 3 feet long, the northern copperhead lives mostly in rocky, wooded areas of the state.

Black Bear

The black bear was nearly extinct in Maryland in the mid-1960s. Today, hundreds of black bears roam Maryland's westernmost counties.

Economy

Ocean City

Ocean City was a sleepy fishing village until the 1870s, when the coming of the railroad transformed it into a bustling resort town.

Tourism

More than 20 million people visit Maryland every year. Many tourists travel to Ocean City, the state's main seaside resort. South of Ocean City in the Atlantic Ocean lies Assateague Island National Seashore. This nearly 40-mile-long island is home to herds of wild horses.

Fort McHenry National Monument is one of Maryland's major historic attractions. Here, in 1814, while watching the British attack the fort during the War of 1812, Francis Scott Key wrote a poem called *The Star-Spangled Banner*, which later became the United States' official national anthem. Another important attraction is Antietam National Battlefield, the site of a bloody Civil War battle. About 23,000 soldiers were killed or wounded at Antietam.

National Aquarium

The daily dolphin show is a main attraction at Baltimore's National Aquarium, which receives visits from about 1.6 million people each year.

Fort McHenry

Designed by a French engineer in 1798, Fort McHenry was built to defend the port of Baltimore.

Annapolis

Graduation ceremonies at the U.S. Naval Academy in Annapolis feature a jet flyover by members of the Blue Angels.

Domino Sugars is one of the largest sugar refineries in the world. The plant in Baltimore, Maryland, has been operating since 1951, and employs more than 1,200 people.

Primary Industries

In the twentieth century, manufacturing became a leading industry in Maryland. Major manufactured products in the state include electric and electronic equipment, food and food products, instruments, chemicals, industrial machinery, and transportation equipment. Printing and publishing and the high-tech sector, including aerospace and biotechnology, are also important to the state's economy.

One of Maryland's leading manufacturing companies is Black & Decker, based in Towson. Black & Decker is a worldwide manufacturer of power tools, hardware, and other home-improvement products. The company supplies products and services to more than 100 countries, and it manufactures products in about a dozen countries.

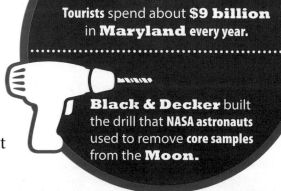

Tourists spend about **$9 billion** in **Maryland** every year.

Black & Decker built the drill that **NASA astronauts** used to remove **core samples** from the **Moon.**

Value of Goods and Services (in Millions of Dollars)

Government accounts for about 18 percent of Maryland's economy. This is a higher percentage than in many other states. What reasons might account for the difference?

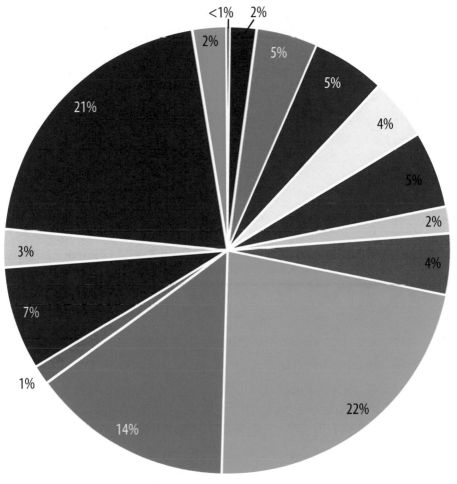

● Agriculture, Forestry, Fishing, Mining............. $1,289	● Finance, Insurance, and Real Estate $76,782
● Utilities $6,436	● Professional and Business Services $50,004
● Construction $15,622	● Education... $4,985
● Manufacturing.. $18,833	● Healthcare and Social Services...................... $25,819
● Wholesale Trade... $15,142	● Hotels and Restaurants $9,039
● Retail Trade.. $18,849	● Government.. $72,149
● Transportation and Warehousing $7,177	● Other Services... $8,441
● Media and Entertainment............................. $14,953	

Oyster season in Maryland runs from October 1 to March 31.

Goods and Services

Maryland's farms produce corn, peanuts, pecans, and soybeans. Maryland's coastal location makes it a prime center for seafood. Crisfield, on the tip of the Eastern Shore, is nicknamed the Seafood Capital of the World. Maryland is the country's top provider of crabs as well as several kinds of fish. Oysters are still an important seafood catch, but pollution and disease have harmed the oyster beds. In the late twentieth century, scientists began efforts to restore oyster beds in Chesapeake Bay.

Farms cover nearly two-fifths of the state's land. Flowers and other **nursery products**, corn, soybeans, and tobacco are particularly important crops. Vegetables are grown and processed on the Eastern Shore. Barley, oats, wheat, and hay are also valuable.

Livestock and livestock products account for about two-thirds of Maryland's farm income. The state is an important producer of **broiler chickens**, which account for more than half of the income from livestock. Maryland farmers also raise cows, hogs, and turkeys.

The service sector, which includes many industries, employs about four-fifths of the state's workers. Many service employees live in Maryland and commute to work in and around Washington, D.C. These employees include federal government workers and military personnel. Among the major institutions that employ Marylanders are the National Institutes of Health, the National Naval Medical Center, the Smithsonian Institution, and the Goddard Space Flight Center.

The National Institute of Health is the main U.S. government medical research agency.

Maryland has one of the best-educated workforces in the country. Almost 40 percent of all Marylanders have a bachelor's degree or higher. The University of Maryland is the main state-sponsored institution for higher learning. It has its main campus at College Park and other branches in Baltimore and Princess Anne. There are 12 state-sponsored schools in total. One of the state's outstanding private higher education and research institutions is Johns Hopkins University in Baltimore. It is well known for its medical school, which has contributed to making Maryland a center of healthcare and medical research.

Johns Hopkins University has been focused on teaching and research for more than 135 years.

History

The Nanticoke were Algonquian-speaking Native Americans who lived along the Chesapeake Bay. Today, they have reservations in Oklahoma and Ontario, Canada.

Native Americans

People hunted in the Maryland area at least 10,000 years ago. By the year 800, Native Americans in Maryland had begun raising crops and hunting with bows and arrows. They established permanent villages by about 1200. Most of the Native Americans in the Maryland region belonged to groups speaking a language in the Algonquian language family. An Iroquoian-speaking group, the Susquehanna, lived along the Susquehanna River.

Native Americans in Maryland hunted deer and other animals and fished the waterways. Agriculture, particularly tobacco, corn, and squash contributed largely to their diet. They also traded blankets and food with other Native American groups in places that are in today's Ohio and New York.

When Europeans first began to settle in the region, the Native Americans established a good relationship. They became fur traders, and helped the Europeans learn to grow native plants, such as tobacco. However, the Native Americans had no defense against European diseases such as smallpox, and their population decreased rapidly. The colonists started to take over Native American lands, and they were forced to move westward.

It is estimated that the Susquehanna numbered between 5,000 to 7,000 people in 1600. By 1700, there were only about 300 Susquehanna in the Maryland area.

Exploring the Land

Although some historians think that the Vikings reached Chesapeake Bay, most believe that Giovanni da Verrazzano was the first European in what is now Maryland. He sailed through the bay in 1524 but did not land in the area. Captain John Smith, a British explorer and a leader of the Jamestown settlement in Virginia, was the first European to map the area, in 1608.

Timeline of Settlement

First Colonies Established

1632 George Calvert, or Lord Baltimore, applies for a charter for the Maryland colony.

1608 Captain John Smith explores and maps the Chesapeake Bay region.

1632 After Lord Baltimore's death, his son Cecilius Calvert receives the Maryland charter.

1524 Giovanni da Verrazzano sails through Chesapeake Bay.

1634 Settlers found St. Mary's City, which becomes the first capital of Maryland.

Early Exploration

At that time, explorers from Great Britain were reaching North America and claiming the shores for their king. The land they claimed included much of Maryland's coast, including Chesapeake Bay. In 1632, King Charles I promised part of the Chesapeake Bay area to George Calvert, or Lord Baltimore, who named the area Maryland in honor of the queen, Henrietta Maria.

Lord Baltimore died before reaching the new world, but his title and mission passed down to his son, Cecilius. Cecilius, or Baron Baltimore, sent his brother Leonard, with about 140 settlers, to North America in November of 1633. They made their first permanent settlement overlooking St. Mary's River.

American Revolutionary War and Civil War

1729 Baltimore is founded near a port that is used for shipping tobacco grown in Maryland.

1695 Annapolis replaces St. Mary's City as the capital of Maryland.

1649 Maryland enacts the first law in the colonies guaranteeing religious freedom for all Christians. Protestants establish the town of Providence, later renamed Annapolis.

Further Settlement

1776 Maryland joins other colonies in declaring independence from Great Britain. Troops from the Maryland Line fight bravely, earning praise from George Washington.

1788 Maryland ratifies the new U.S. Constitution and becomes the 7th state on April 28.

1861–1862 Although slavery is legal in the state, Maryland chooses not to join the Confederacy. The state becomes an important battleground in the early years of the Civil War.

The Yaocomico and Piscataway groups helped the early European settlers of Maryland develop survival skills.

The First Settlers

At first, the settlers who arrived from Great Britain with Lord Baltimore's son, Leonard, enjoyed good harvests and established strong ties with the Native Americans in the area of St. Mary's City. The Native Americans traded furs and food for **textiles** and tools. They also helped the settlers grow corn. This assistance prevented the European newcomers from starving. The settlers also grew tobacco, which they sold to Great Britain. Using the money they made selling tobacco, the settlers established **plantations** to grow even more of the crop.

Religious freedom remained an important part of Maryland. By the mid-1600s, Puritans were beginning to settle in the area of Maryland and wanted to remove the original laws guaranteeing religious freedom. In 1655, there was a small civil war within Maryland when a group of Puritans took control of the colony. This resulted in the son of Lord Baltimore losing all of his property rights in the area.

In the mid-1700s, Great Britain and France went to war for control of eastern North America. To pay for the war, Great Britain taxed settlers heavily on goods imported from Europe, including sugar, tea, and newspapers. This angered the settlers. In 1774, a year after the Boston Tea Party, colonists burned a ship loaded with tea at an Annapolis dock.

The high taxes led the colonists to stop buying from Great Britain and to fight for independence. By 1776, the American Revolutionary War had swept across the colonies, and Marylanders took an active part. A group of soldiers called the Maryland Line joined the Continental Army. In 1776, four representatives from Maryland signed the Declaration of Independence.

During the American Revolutionary War, most soldiers were self taught. They originally had civilian jobs, such as merchants, lawyers, and farmers.

Samuel Chase, William Paca, Thomas Stone, and Charles Carroll signed the Declaration of Independence as representatives of Maryland.

History Makers

Located on the dividing line between the North and South, Maryland has been home to many leaders in the fight for equal rights. Some of those who have called Maryland their home include a pioneering congresswoman, and a supreme court justice. Others are influential writers, the founders of several well-known companies, and even a saint.

Elizabeth Ann Seton (1774-1821)

Elizabeth Ann Seton was the first native-born American to be named as a saint by the Catholic Church. She was born in New York City and became a Catholic in 1805. She devoted the rest of her life to teaching and helping the poor. In 1809, she founded a religious community, the Sisters of Charity, in Emmitsburg, Maryland, where she died in 1821. The Catholic Church declared her a saint in 1975.

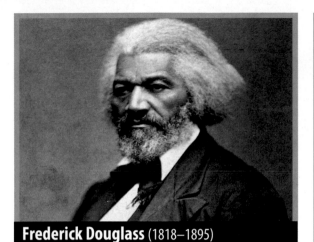

Frederick Douglass (1818–1895)

Born to a slave woman on the Eastern Shore, Frederick Douglass grew up both in rural Maryland and in Baltimore. After he was treated cruelly by a slavemaster, he escaped to New York City in 1838. He spent the rest of his life speaking and writing against the evils of slavery. His most famous book was his *Narrative of the Life of Frederick Douglass, an American Slave, Written by Himself* (1845).

Harriet Tubman (c. 1820–1913)

Harriet Tubman was born into slavery in Maryland's Dorchester County. She worked hard to end slavery, risking her life to help more than 300 slaves escape to freedom through the Underground Railroad. During the Civil War, this brave woman worked as a nurse, a cook, and a spy.

Thurgood Marshall (1908–1993)

Born in Baltimore, Thurgood Marshall graduated at the top of his class in law school. As a lawyer for the NAACP, he argued for equal rights for all U.S. citizens. He convinced the Supreme Court to outlaw the practice in many states of forcing African American and Caucasian children to attend separate schools. In 1967, Marshall became the first African American to serve on the Supreme Court.

Nancy Pelosi (1940–)

Nancy Pelosi comes from one of Baltimore's leading political families. Her father and brother both served as mayor of Baltimore. Pelosi moved to California, where she won election to the U.S. House of Representatives. From 2007 through 2010, she was speaker of the House, the first woman ever to hold that high office.

Culture

Annapolis is located on the Chesapeake Bay. The city has almost 40,000 residents.

About 63 percent of Baltimore's population is African American. Slightly more than 30 percent are of European descent.

The People Today

Maryland has quite a large population for such a small state. At the time of the 2010 Census, Maryland had a population of nearly 5.8 million people, making it the 19th most populous state in the country. Between 2000 and 2010, Maryland's population grew by 9 percent, slightly less than the national average.

About four-fifths of Maryland's population lives along a strip of land that runs between Baltimore and Washington, D.C. Baltimore is Maryland's largest city as well as the center of most of its cultural and recreational activities. Dundalk is a large suburb of Baltimore.

Maryland also maintains a strong rural tradition, especially in the western part of the state. Smaller cities and towns in these areas enjoy many of the same conveniences as larger cities. They grew along railroad tracks and canals, and are now popular tourist sites for people who live in cities.

Maryland's population more than **doubled** between **1950** and **2010.** However, population in Baltimore **decreased.**

Q What are some reasons for this population shift?

State Government

Maryland's government consists of three branches. The General Assembly, the state's legislative branch, passes the state's laws. The General Assembly has two chambers, or parts. They are a 47-member Senate and a 141-member House of Delegates. Members of both chambers are elected to four-year terms. Among the laws passed by the legislature was one in 1939 making "Maryland, My Maryland" the official state song. James Ryder Randall wrote the words to this song in April 1861, at the beginning of the Civil War. Randall wanted Maryland to side with the Confederacy, and he felt outrage when Union troops entered Baltimore.

The Maryland State House, where the Maryland General Assembly convenes, is the oldest continually used state capitol building in the country.

The person responsible for carrying out the laws is the governor, who heads the state's executive branch and also serves a four-year term. Other elected members of the executive branch include the lieutenant governor, the attorney general, and the state **comptroller**.

The judicial branch is responsible for interpreting the state's laws. The state's highest court is the Court of Appeals. Judges are appointed by the governor, but must be reelected in the next election cycle if they wish to keep their positions. They serve 10-year terms.

Larry Hogan is the 62nd governor of Maryland.

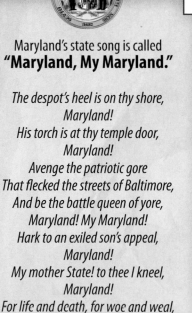

Maryland's state song is called **"Maryland, My Maryland."**

The despot's heel is on thy shore,
Maryland!
His torch is at thy temple door,
Maryland!
Avenge the patriotic gore
That flecked the streets of Baltimore,
And be the battle queen of yore,
Maryland! My Maryland!
Hark to an exiled son's appeal,
Maryland!
My mother State! to thee I kneel,
Maryland!
For life and death, for woe and weal,
Thy peerless chivalry reveal,
And gird thy beauteous limbs with steel,
Maryland! My Maryland!
* excerpted

Baltimore's St. Patrick's Day parade has been an annual event to celebrate Irish-Americans for more than 50 years.

Celebrating Culture

Many Marylanders are of British or French **ancestry**. Settlers from other countries began arriving in the region in the 1700s. Germans settled near Frederick and then around Baltimore in the 1730s. Many Marylanders continue to celebrate traditional German customs and festivals, such as Oktoberfest.

Baltimore is a very diverse city, with people of many different national backgrounds. The largest groups include people of German, British, Irish, or Italian descent, and people of Polish, Czech, Greek, and Russian descent also live in the city. Neighborhoods throughout Baltimore help to preserve these distinctive European traditions.

In the twentieth and early twenty-first centuries, Maryland received many immigrants from Asia and Latin America, adding to the state's cultural richness. Marylanders born outside of the United States make up 14 percent of the state's population. About 9 percent are Hispanic or Latino, and almost 6.5 percent are of Asian descent.

African Americans are the state's largest minority group. Many African Americans in Maryland trace their ancestry from slaves who lived in the state. At the time of the first U.S. Census, slaves made up about one of every three state residents. After the Civil War, former slaves from the South moved north to Baltimore, where they joined a well-established community of African Americans who had been free for several generations. Today, nearly two-thirds of Baltimore residents and about 30 percent of all Marylanders are African American.

The African American Festival in Baltimore is the largest cultural festival on the East Coast.

Maryland has no federally recognized Native American groups, and Native Americans make up less than 1 percent of the state's population. Maryland hosts several annual powwows and other cultural events that celebrate Native American culture with traditional dancing, singing, crafts, and food. Yearly festivals include the Howard County Powwow and the Native American Heritage Day Powwow in Silver Spring.

The Healing Horse Spirit Powwow in Mt. Airy, Maryland, acts as a cultural event and fundraiser for horse rescue organizations.

Joan Jett grew up in Rockville, Maryland. She received her first guitar when she was still in junior high school.

Arts and Entertainment

Maryland has produced many popular writers. Born in Baltimore in 1947, Tom Clancy published his first novel, *The Hunt for Red October*, in 1984. Like many of Clancy's later works, this "techno-thriller" blends suspense and modern technology with the world of politics. Many of Clancy's novels have been made into successful Hollywood films. Another well-known Maryland novelist is Dashiell Hammett, who was born in St. Mary's County in 1894. His detective stories, such as *The Maltese Falcon* and *The Thin Man*, thrilled and captivated readers.

The journalist and critic H. L. Mencken, a native of Baltimore, also gained a national reputation. He wrote essays about literature and about what he considered the faults of life in the United States. His book *The American Language*, first published in 1919, is considered a classic.

Born in **Baltimore** in **1940**, composer and guitarist **Frank Zappa** was inducted into the **Rock and Roll Hall of Fame** in **1995**.

The popular musical **Hairspray,** winner of eight Tony Awards, is set in 1962 Baltimore.

Maryland boasts many fine art museums, including the Baltimore Museum of Art. Founded in 1914, the museum is the largest in Maryland. Its collections include more than 85,000 objects from around the world and a library with about 50,000 books and magazines.

Classical music lovers in Maryland flock to the Joseph Meyerhoff Symphony Hall, home of the Baltimore Symphony Orchestra, and to the Lyric Opera House, also in Baltimore. The Maryland Hall for the Creative Arts, in Annapolis, showcases a variety of performing arts, including classical music, opera, and ballet.

Billie Holiday was born in Philadelphia, Pennsylvania, but grew up in Baltimore.

Many musicians have also called Maryland home. Billie Holiday is one of the most popular jazz musicians of all time. While she made her mark in New York City in the late 1920s, she never forgot her Baltimore home. Holiday's singing influenced musicians for decades to come, and her distinctive style was often imitated but rarely matched. Two more recent performers, Joan Jett and Tori Amos, grew up in Maryland.

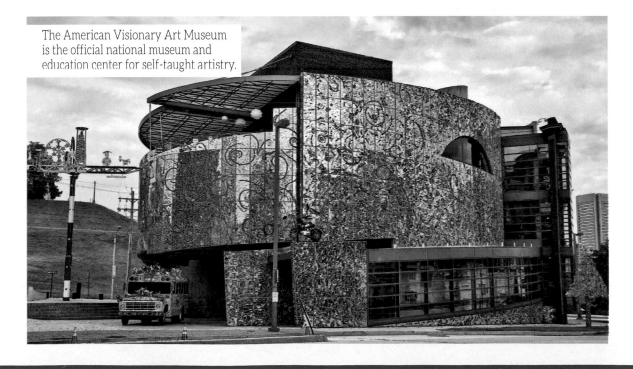

The American Visionary Art Museum is the official national museum and education center for self-taught artistry.

Sports and Recreation

Maryland residents and vacationers alike enjoy sailing, fishing, duck and goose hunting, skiing, and whitewater rafting. Calvert Cliffs is a popular spot for beachcombing, and the Appalachian Trail is good for hiking. With its long shoreline, Chesapeake Bay is a popular summer tourist attraction.

Equestrian sports are popular with Marylanders. One of these is jousting. In modern jousting contests, competitors race their horses down an 80-yard track to spear three rings with their lances. Another popular Maryland pastime is horse racing. The Preakness, held in Baltimore, is one of the most famous racing events in the country. It is one of the three horse races that make up the **Triple Crown**.

The first Preakness was held in 1873. Today, attendance for the race is second only to the Kentucky Derby.

After developing his swimming skills at the North Baltimore Aquatic Club, **Michael Phelps** went on to become the most-decorated Olympian with **22 medals**.

Maryland chose **jousting** as the **state sport** in **1962**.

Lacrosse, played with a stick with a netted basket, is a fast-paced, exciting sport that is very popular in Maryland. The lacrosse teams from Johns Hopkins University and the University of Maryland are generally among the best in the country. Since 1891, the Johns Hopkins Blue Jays have won 44 national championships.

The University of Maryland women's lacrosse team won the 2015 NCAA women's championships.

The state has several major professional sports teams. In Major League Baseball, the Baltimore Orioles play their games in Oriole Park at Camden Yards. From 1982 until 1998, Oriole infielder Cal Ripken, Jr. did not miss a game, setting a record of 2,632 consecutive games played. Ripken continued to impress fans with his hitting and fielding until his retirement after the 2001 season. He was inducted into the Baseball Hall of Fame in 2007.

In 1984, Maryland sports fans were crushed when the Baltimore Colts professional football team left Maryland for Indianapolis. The National Football League returned to the state in 1996 when the Baltimore Ravens played their first season. In 2001, the Ravens won the Super Bowl by beating the New York Giants, 34–7.

The Baltimore Ravens won the Super Bowl in 2012 under coach John Harbaugh.

Get To Know
MARYLAND

The Baltimore Ravens are named after the famous poem, *THE RAVEN*, by Edgar Allan Poe.

The *Maryland Gazette*, founded in 1727, is the **oldest continuously-running newspaper** in the country.

About **one** in **five** Marylanders works for a local, state, or federal **government agency**.

The **first female professor** of medicine was employed by John Hopkins University in 1901.

White's Ferry, between Virginia and Maryland, is the only ferry that regularly crosses the Potomac River.

Maryland has more than 50 state parks and forests.

St. Mary's City is home to an 800-acre **living history** museum containing recreations of a tobacco plantation, the state house, and one of the first ships that brought European settlers to the state.

Brain Teasers

What have you learned about Maryland after reading this book? Test your knowledge by answering these questions. All of the information can be found in the text you just read. The answers are provided below for easy reference.

1 In what year did Leonard Calvert land in Maryland?

2 How many federally recognized Native American groups are there in Maryland?

3 How many species of venomous snakes live in Maryland?

4 What percentage of the state is covered by forests?

5 When did Maryland enter the Union?

6 In what Maryland city was the Treaty of Paris, which granted the colonies independence, signed?

7 What is the official state bird?

8 In what year did jousting become the official state sport?

ANSWER KEY
1. 1634 2. None 3. Two 4. 40 percent
5. April 28, 1788, as the 7th state 6. Annapolis
7. The Baltimore oriole 8. 1962

Key Words

ancestry: people from whom an individual or group is descended

broiler chickens: young chickens raised for meat rather than eggs

comptroller: official who reviews government income and spending

diversity: variety

endangered species: a kind of animal or plant that is in danger of completely dying out

estuary: the part of a river where it meets the sea, where fresh and salt water mix

hydroelectric: using waterpower to create electricity

nursery products: commercially grown plants

plantations: large estates that grow crops such as cotton, tea, and tobacco

textiles: fabrics made by weaving or knitting

Triple Crown: the title held by the horse that wins the Kentucky Derby, the Preakness, and the Belmont Stakes races

wetlands: swamps and marshes

Index

Log on to www.av2books.com

AV² by Weigl brings you media enhanced books that support active learning. Go to www.av2books.com, and enter the special code found on page 2 of this book. You will gain access to enriched and enhanced content that supplements and complements this book. Content includes video, audio, weblinks, quizzes, a slide show, and activities.

AV² Online Navigation

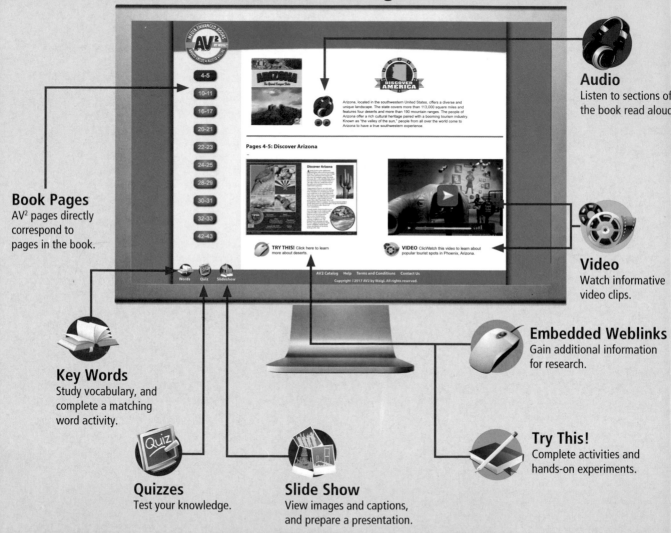

Audio
Listen to sections of the book read aloud

Book Pages
AV² pages directly correspond to pages in the book.

Video
Watch informative video clips.

Key Words
Study vocabulary, and complete a matching word activity.

Embedded Weblinks
Gain additional information for research.

Try This!
Complete activities and hands-on experiments.

Quizzes
Test your knowledge.

Slide Show
View images and captions, and prepare a presentation.

AV² was built to bridge the gap between print and digital. We encourage you to tell us what you like and what you want to see in the future.

Sign up to be an AV² Ambassador at www.av2books.com/ambassador.

Due to the dynamic nature of the Internet, some of the URLs and activities provided as part of AV² by Weigl may have changed or ceased to exist. AV² by Weigl accepts no responsibility for any such changes. All media enhanced books are regularly monitored to update addresses and sites in a timely manner. Contact AV² by Weigl at 1-866-649-3445 or av2books@weigl.com with any questions, comments, or feedback.